PEN & BRUSH
The Author as Artist

I

William Makepeace Thackeray

II

William Blake to Denton Welch

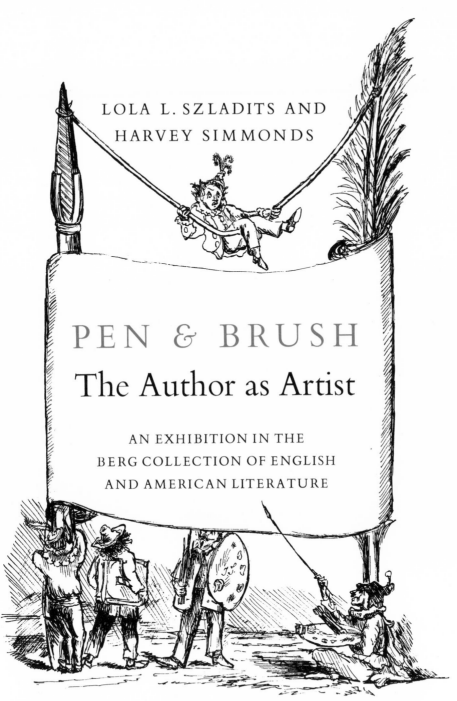

LOLA L. SZLADITS AND
HARVEY SIMMONDS

PEN & BRUSH

The Author as Artist

AN EXHIBITION IN THE
BERG COLLECTION OF ENGLISH
AND AMERICAN LITERATURE

THE NEW YORK PUBLIC LIBRARY
Astor, Lenox and Tilden Foundations

THIS CATALOGUE OF AN EXHIBITION IN THE BERG COLLECTION
IS PRODUCED WITH THE ASSISTANCE OF THE
JUDGE AND MRS SAMUEL D. LEVY MEMORIAL PUBLICATION FUND

On the front cover: item 27
On the title page: anonymous pen and ink sketch
On the back cover: item 138

INTRODUCTION

THIS EXHIBITION might well have been entitled *Incidental Art*. It might have been entitled *Portrait of the Author as a Young Artist*. And it might have been entitled *Scribblers and Doodlers*: all would fit the occasion. Certainly, the art is incidental in terms of the holdings of the Berg Collection. In margins, in letters, in notebooks, authors have drawn, doodled, and dreamt of themselves as artists. Some great names are missing, Wyndham Lewis and D. H. Lawrence among them; the Pre-Raphaelites are missing. Some authors, who are also artists in their own right (Blake, Kipling, Beerbohm) are sparsely represented as artists in the Collection, devoted as it principally is to literature.

The artist in most cases emerged young. Tennyson drew for his governess at fourteen; Maurice Baring did so a century later at a very much younger age. Chesterton, Hardy, Rosenberg had formal art training, as did the author-artist William Makepeace Thackeray, a practicing professional in both fields who occupies the prominent position in this exhibition. The Berg Collection has one of the world's outstanding Thackeray libraries, which includes a strongly representative selection from the thousands of sketches for cartoons in periodicals, illustrations for his own works, and pleasantly ephemeral pictorial letters and marginalia.

One could engage in pedestrian psychology, speculating on the hidden meanings, frustrated drives, and sublimated desires expressed in some of the incidental art exhibited. The subconscious undoubtedly emerges in doodles or elaborate drawings which reflect the author reflecting upon his face, his work, his thoughts. We feel no special competence in that field, and prefer to offer this catalogue to our visitors in the spirit in which it was compiled: each new discovery, with its suggestion of the complicated interaction of the mind and the hand, was a particular delight.

2

PART I

William Makepeace Thackeray

(1811 – 1863)

THE PORTRAITIST

I

HE stood six foot three tall. He had dark, curling hair, a pair of quick, twinkling eyes which, for nearsightedness, required glasses at an early age. A youthful fistfight led to a broken nose, the reason for his choice of the first part of the pseudonym by which the reading public knew him throughout his career: Michael Angelo Titmarsh. His head was a little too large, covered in later years by a shock of white hair. He was rotund to the point of obesity toward the end of his life, and his American friend John Lothrop Motley recorded impressions of a "colossal infant, smooth, white, shiny ringlety hair, flaxen, alas, with advancing years, a roundish face, with a little dab of a nose upon which it is a perpetual wonder how he keeps his spectacles." Those spectacles and a miniature self-portrait caricature as jester had become his signature.

If we had only the visual record Thackeray the artist made of himself our impression would match Motley's. Like other and greater artists before him, Thackeray found that the best study of faces was the study of his own. His features appear even in his work as illustrator; the "colossal infant" re-emerges in the most unexpected places. He recorded himself in his varied roles: student, theatre-goer, young swain, law clerk, husband, father, traveler, lecturer—and again and again in the guise of Michael Angelo Titmarsh, who bore such a close resemblance to Mr Punch.

The twin threads of author and artist were intertwined in Thackeray's career to form an exceptionally strong and colorful fabric. As artist and as author he was a realist, a humorist, and a social critic. Early academic studies in Paris and an observant eye served Thackeray exceptionally well in his work as sensitive portraitist. In his portraits life is caught at its most appealing and most vulnerable moments, often in some way domestic or familial. This highly characteristic quality is linked to the artist's frequent choice of those he knew or loved to serve as models for his illustrations, as they did for the characters in the author's novels.

1. Self-caricature as a jester.
Pencil. 1 ¾ × 1 ½ inches.
Signed with initials in the lower right corner.

2. Self-portrait.
Pencil. 6 × 4 ½ inches.
Mounted and bound with the manuscript of his poem "Our Drama Ends."

3. "Ip Ip Urray."

Pen and ink. 7¼×4½ inches.

Dated September 30 1861 in an unidentified hand.

This caricature bears a faint resemblance to the youthful Thackeray.

4. "Myself of course as I appeared at 18 years of age."

Pen and ink. 7¼×4½ inches.

5. "Here am I sitting on a high stool in a special pleaders office . . . ." Self-caricature.

Pen and ink. 2¼×2¼ inches.

At head of autograph letter to Edward Fitzgerald; Temple, [London, n d].

6. Self-caricature.

Pen and ink. 6¾×5 inches.

On the half title of Lady Rachel Russell's copy of *The Kickleburys on the Rhine*, London 1850, inscribed "with Mr. Titmarsh's compliments."

6

7

7. "Mr. Michael Angelo Titmarsh as he appeared at Willis' Rooms in his celebrated character of Mr. Thackeray." Self-caricature.

Pencil. 6¼×5¼ inches.

Thackeray gave his tremendously popular lectures on *The English Humourists of the Eighteenth Century* in 1851, at Willis' Rooms, King Street, St James's.

8. "Bulwer's boots are very fine in the accompanying masterly design. Remark the traces of emotion on the cheeks of the author (the notorious WMT) . . . ." Self-caricature.

Pen and ink. 3¼×2½ inches.

In autograph letter to Mary Holmes; Kensington, [London, March 5 1852].

9. "Before I go to Richmond early early in the morning tomorrow, I must pay a many debts w^h I owe here and one of them is a pleasant little debt indeed: to a poor young lady by the name of Miss Lucy whose back I hope is better by this time; and whose kind little hand I hereby respectfully salute." Self-caricature.

Pen and ink. ¾×1 inch.

In autograph letter to Lucy Baxter; "Febbywerry" 26 [1853].

10. "I go down on my knees to you and beg you to read my queer petition." Self-caricature.

Pen and ink. 3¼×2¼ inches.

At head of autograph letter to the Honorable Miss Campbell; Onslow Square, [London, June 13 1861].

11. "My foot was actually uplifted to quit the shore of Albion . . . ." Two self-caricatures.

Pen and ink. Each 7 1/4 × 4 1/2 inches.

In autograph letter to Sir William and Lady Knighton; Kensington, [London], July 20 [1863].

My dear Sir and Madam

My foot was actually uplifted to quit the shore of Albion, when the morning's post brought your obleeging invitation which instant

caused me to turn back again. We shall be delighted to come to you for Goodwood. As for the Cup, your best Claret I daresay is good enough for me,

13

12. Michelangelo. Study for decorative initial.

Pencil. 3 ¾ × 2 inches.

Signed with initials at the upper left. Mounted and bound in a copy of his *The Virginians*, v 2, London 1859, facing the corresponding plate, preceding p [65].

13. Isabella Shawe Thackeray.

Water color. 4 ½ × 4 inches.

"The most amiable & gentle of women," wrote Mrs Thackeray's sister on the verso of this portrait.

14. "This is most awful. The girls are sitting before me, and I was trying to draw them but the pen and the perspective & the clumsiness & position of the artist don't admit of doing it." Portrait of Anne Isabella, "Anny," later Lady Ritchie, and Harriet Marian, "Minny," later Mrs Leslie Stephen.

Pen and ink. 2 ¼ × 3 ¾ inches.

In autograph letter to Mrs George Baxter; Rome, December 17 [1853].

15. Self-portrait, with other portraits, including those of George Cruikshank, Charles Dickens, William Henry Brookfield, and Mrs Brookfield.

Pencil with oil on ivory. Five leaves (recto and verso, two versos blank). Each 3 × 1 ¾ inches.

Thackeray's monogram in silver mounted on the ivory cover.

16. Jane Brookfield.

Pencil with crayon. 5 ¾ × 4 ¼ inches.

Mounted in an album kept by Mrs Brookfield and presented by her to Kate Perry, November 27 1854.

17. Mrs Samuel Lover.
Pencil. 5×4 inches.
Dated Dublin, 1843 in an unidentified hand.

18. Prince Albert.
Pencil. $6\frac{1}{4} \times 3\frac{3}{4}$ inches.
On verso of the manuscript of six verses of his poem "The Pimlico Pavilion."

Prince Albert of Flandthers, that chief of Commandthers
    On whom my best blessing hereby I bestow,
With goold & vermillion has decked that pavillion,
    Where the Queen may take tay in her sweet Pimlico.

19. William Kenworthy Browne.
Pencil with water color. $8\frac{3}{4} \times 6$ inches.
Dated "about 1840" on verso by Edward Fitz-gerald.

20. Goethe.
Pencil with pen and ink. $6\frac{1}{2} \times 3\frac{1}{2}$ inches.
Signed with initials in the lower right corner.
Thackeray met Goethe in Weimar in 1830.

21. Three portrait sketches of unidentified subjects.
Pen and ink with wash.
$8\frac{1}{2} \times 6$ inches.
Signed with initials in the lower right corner.
8×5 inches.
Signed with initials in the lower right corner.
$9 \times 7\frac{1}{4}$ inches.
Signed with initials in the lower left corner.

22. "King of the Garrick Club." Portrait sketch of unidentified subject.
Pen and ink. $3\frac{1}{2} \times 3$ inches.
At head of undated autograph letter to John Leech.

22

THE CARICATURIST

"I HAVE come to the conclusion that whenever he writes Mephistopheles stands on his right hand and Raphael on his left; the great Doubter and Sneerer usually guides the pen, the Angel noble and gentle interlines letters of light here and there . . ." wrote Charlotte Brontë, who in 1847 dedicated the second edition of *Jane Eyre* to "the satirist of 'Vanity Fair.'"

The portraitist and the caricaturist are so closely allied in Thackeray that at times he found it necessary to remark that a drawing was not intended to be a caricature. He is at his best in the fast, humorous sketches which resulted in his first published work, *Flore et Zephyr* (1836). As a contributor to *Punch* and *Fraser's Magazine* he established himself professionally both as journalist and illustrator. He reviewed annual exhibitions of paintings in a series of articles entitled "Strictures on Pictures," the pictorial trace of which can be seen in whimsical caricatures of art patrons contemplating art. Characters from all walks of life, Cockneys and snobs, actors, the military, and those fanciful creatures whose semi-realism justified their existence in such works as *The Rose and the Ring* (1854), crowd his finished work and the countless embellished letters and fragments distributed among his circle.

23. "Frontispiece. 'Mentor looking with an eye of Benevolent Complacency on the well-directed labors of Youth.' "

Pen and ink. 10 ¼ × 8 ½ inches.

On verso of the front cover of a school notebook entitled "Algebra," and signed "WILLIAM M. THACKERAY, July 1829." This is an early exercise in wishful thinking by one who was weak in mathematics.

24. "Here is a scene at the Spotted dog a publick house near the Strand where you pay tuppence to hear singing etc. The faces are not at all caricatured not even the eyebrows."

Pen and ink with water color. 4 × 7 ¼ inches.

At head of undated letter to Edward Fitzgerald.

25. "How Graf Otto von Blumenbach leads from the altar his lovely bride Ottilie, Amelie, Melanie, Jenny von Rosenthal." One of seventeen cartoon sketches.

Pen and ink. 8 × 6 ¾ inches.

These amusing drawings were made at Weimar about 1830 for Caroline Vavasour, a young girl whose parents were then living there.

26. "Mademoiselle LÉOCADIE rôle de Lycoris; BOHÉMOND rôle de Pygmalion dans le ballet de ce nom."

Pencil. 7 ¼ × 10 inches.

This sketch closely resembles Thackeray's first published lithographs, the series entitled *Flore et Zephyr*, which affectionately mocked ballet attitudes.

27. At the art exhibition.

Pen and ink with white wash. 3 ¾ × 3 ¾ inches.

Signed with initials in the lower left corner.

28. " 'A Pack of Nonsense' by Mr. Punch."

Nine playing cards embellished with caricatures. Each 3 ½ × 2 ¼ inches.

29. The royal family.

Pen and ink and mounted postage stamps. 5 × 6 ¾ inches.

30. "Paris Sketches." Sketch for the frontispiece of *The Paris Sketch Book*, 1840.

Pen and ink. 7¼×4½ inches.

31. "Dinner-giving snobs further considered." Pencil with pen and ink. 4¾×3¼ inches.

Signed with initials at the center left and with spectacles at the center right. In the first edition of *The Book of Snobs*, London 1848, this drawing embellishes the initial "I."

30

Explanation of the Allegory.

Number 1's an ancient Carlist, number 3 a Paris Artist,
Gloomily there stands between them, number 2 a Bonapartist,
In the middle is King Louis Philippe standing at his ease,
Guarded by a loyal grocer, & a serjeant of Police,
4's the People in a passion, 6 a Priest of pious mien,
5 a gentleman of Fashion, copied from a Magazine.

36

My dear Dr Primrose

Lest I should be too much elated by your praises
the other day see what a wholesome corrective was in
store for me in that heap of letters wh. you saw

32. "Anteros" and "Eros."
Pencil with water color. Each 3 × 2 ¼ inches.
Signed on the mount.

33. "A Pot-poet."
Pencil. 2 × 2 ¾ inches.
Marginal drawing in Thackeray's copy of *Microcosmography* by John Earle, London 1811, p 80.

34. "Are you not a man, and my Brother?";
"Howadjee" [George W. Curtis]; and "Longfellow."
Pen and ink. 1 ½ × 1 ¼ inches; 1 ¼ × 1 ¼ inches;
7 ½ × 1 inches.
Drawn by Thackeray on the cover of a copy of *Putnam's Monthly* (January 1853) during his first visit to America.

35. "English Humourists of the last Century by
✗✗✗ ."
Water color. 3 ¾ × 4 inches.
Mounted, facing p [1] in a copy of *The English Humourists of the Eighteenth Century*, second edition, London 1853, presented by Thackeray to W. W. F. Synge.

36. Messenger delivering a letter to Dr Primrose.
Pen and ink. 3 ¼ × 3 ¾ inches.
At head of autograph letter to the Rev Whitwell Elwin; [London, June 1861]. The eccentric character of the recipient of this letter, Thackeray's friend in later years, earned him the affectionate alias of Dr Primrose.

37. "The more Heads the better."
Pen and ink. 7¼×4 inches.
Signed with initials in the lower right corner.

38. "A Portrait of some one unborn."
Pen and ink. 7½×6 inches.
Signed with initials in the lower right corner.

39. "Literature presenting Science to Britannia."
Pen and ink. 5½×7 inches.

40. Carriage ride.
Pen and ink with water color. 5×7½ inches.

41. Betsinda and Prince Bilbo. Sketch of characters for *The Rose and the Ring*.
Pencil. 4×5¾ inches.
Signed with initials in the lower right corner.

42. Two character sketches for *The Rose and the Ring*.
Water color. Each 3½×2¼ inches.

43. "A Trifle from Titmarsh."
Pen and colored inks. 4¼×3 inches.

43

THE ILLUSTRATOR

IT TOOK Thackeray some time to discover his vocation. He left Cambridge without graduating, experienced the tedium of the legal profession, owned a newspaper, and lost most of his fortune. Early praise for his drawing and the memory of youthful visits to Paris prompted the happy decision to study art in the French capital. Liberated from the oppression of money he frequented Bohemian circles, spent his evenings at the theatre and ballet, and met Isabella Shawe, whom he married in 1836. The necessity to support her and their two surviving daughters—one child died in infancy—determined his future career.

The workload was tremendous. Fond of harking back to his old acquaintances and surroundings, Thackeray drew on people and stories from his school days, domestic experiences, and foreign travels; his were the observations of the ever-watchful social critic. The Christmas books *Mrs. Perkins's Ball* (1846), *Our Street* (1847), *Dr. Birch and His Young Friends* (1848), *Rebecca and Rowena* (1849), and finally *The Rose and the Ring* (1854) supplied Thackeray the illustrator with stories told by Thackeray the occasional writer. The novelist at work on his major successes, *Vanity Fair* (1847–1848), *The History of Pendennis* (1848–1850), and *The Virginians* (1858–1859), provided new matter for the imagination of the artist. One contemplates with wonder the creative energy this master put into his work while family problems and personal disasters preoccupied the man. The lecture tours which brought him to the United States from 1852 to 1853 and again from 1855 to 1856 partly restored the financial security he had lost in his youth and added to the great popular success that accompanied him to the grave. Shortly before his sudden and unexpected death he relinquished his post as editor of the *Cornhill Magazine*, to which he had contributed his last illustrated works.

Veracious History of Dionysius Diddler

44. "This is Dionysius Diddler!"
Pencil with pen and ink. 9 ½ × 6 ½ inches.
On p 2 of the manuscript, dated "1838–9," as prepared for publication in the *Whitey-brown Paper Magazine*.

45. "And upon me honour and conshience, now I'm dthressed; but I look intirely ginteel."
Pen and ink with water color. 8 ¾ × 6 ½ inches.
Signed with initials in the lower left corner. Bound with proofs of Thackeray's contributions to the *Autographic Mirror*, 1864–1866.

47

Mrs. Perkins's Ball

46. "The Banquet Hall deserted; Mr. Mulligan entirely refuses to go home." Study for the illustration accompanying the text ". . . everybody was gone; but the abominable Mulligan sate swinging his legs at the lonely supper-table."
Water color. 6 ¾ × 5 ½ inches.

47. "This is Mr. Hicks the poet . . . ." Study for the illustration accompanying the text "Hicks was taken in an inspired attitude, regarding the chandelier, and pretending he didn't know that Miss Pettifer was looking at him."
Pencil with water color. 7 × 4 ½ inches.
Mounted and bound in a copy of his *Mrs. Perkins's Ball*, London [1847] facing the corresponding plate, preceding p [19]—plate reproduced above, right.

Doctor Birch and His Young Friends

48. "Slogger Major and Slogger Minor." Study for "The Dear Brothers."
Pencil with wash. 8 ½ × 6 ¼ inches.

49. "Brown; Jones; Robinson; Boxall Major; Boxall Minor; Tiffin Minimus." Study for "The Dear Brothers."
Pencil. 6 × 5 inches.

50. "Take him up." Study for "The Last Boy of All."
Pencil. 8 ¾ × 5 ¾ inches.

51. Study for "Who Stole the Jam."
Pencil with wash. 5 ½ × 4 inches.

Vanity Fair

52. Study for "The Letter before Waterloo."
Pen and ink. 7½×6 inches.
Signed with initials in the lower left corner.

53. Study for "The Letter before Waterloo."
Pencil with water color. 8×5 inches.
Signed in the lower left corner. Mounted and bound in a copy of his *Vanity Fair*, London 1848, facing the corresponding plate, the frontispiece.

54. Study for "Mr. Joseph Entangled."
Pencil. 5×4 inches.

55. "Thanks to a fashionable tailor Captain Osborne made a pretty genteel appearance."
Pen and ink with water color. 6½×5 inches.
Thackeray made this drawing for sale at a bazaar, and accompanied it with a pseudo-quotation from *Vanity Fair*.

54

The History of Pendennis

56. "A." Sketch for decorative initial for Volume 1, Chapter 3.

Pen and ink. 8½×5¼ inches.

Inscribed "Drawn by W. M. Thackeray" by his daughter Anne, Lady Ritchie.

57. Study for "The General's Salutation of the Major."

Pencil with water color. 6½×4½ inches.

Signed in the lower left corner. Mounted and bound in a copy of his *The History of Pendennis*, v 1, London 1850, facing the corresponding plate, following p 96.

58. Study for "The General's Salutation of the Major."

Pen and ink with water color. 7¾×5¼ inches.

Signed with initials in the lower right corner. Mounted, facing p 96 of a copy of his *The History of Pendennis*, Part 3, London January 1849.

59. Study for the illustration accompanying the text "As for Pen's gravity, it was sorely put to the test . . . ."

Pencil with water color. 6×4¾ inches.

Signed with initials in the lower left corner. Mounted and bound in a copy of his *The History of Pendennis*, v 2, London 1850, facing the corresponding plate, p 18.

60. "Colonel Alamont [i.e. Altamont] Refuses to Move on."

Pencil with water color. 8¼×5¼ inches.

Signed in the lower left corner. Thackeray here portrays himself as the Colonel.

The Virginians

61. Character sketches.
Pen and ink. 7¼×5¼ inches.

62. Study for "Behind Montague House."
Pencil with water color. 7×5 inches.

63. "H." Sketch for decorative initial for Volume 1, Chapter 3.

Pencil with pen and ink. 7×5 inches.

Signed in the lower right corner. Mounted and bound in a copy of his *The Virginians*, v 1, London 1858–1859, facing the corresponding plate, p [20].

64. "W" and "M." Studies for decorative initials for Volume 2, Chapters 4 and 8.

Pencil. Each 3½×2½ inches.

Mounted, facing the corresponding plates, p [27] and [54] in a copy of his *The Virginians*, Parts 13 and 14, London 1858.

65. Study for "A Dancing Lesson."

Pencil with pen and ink. 8½×5½ inches.

Signed in the lower right corner. Bound in a copy of his *The Virginians*, v 1, London 1858–1859, facing the corresponding plate, following p 108.

Novels by Eminent Hands, and Character Sketches

66. Study to accompany the text " 'CORBLEU! What a lovely creature that was in the Fitzbattle-axe box to-night,' said one of a group of young dandies who were leaning over the velvet-cushioned balconies of the Coventry Club . . . ."

Pencil with pen and ink. 6½×4½ inches.

Signed with initials at lower center. Mounted and bound in a copy of his *Novels by Eminent Hands, and Character Sketches*, London 1856, facing p 37.

The Four Georges

67. Studies for illustrations of Lord North, Mr Fox, Mr Pitt, and Mr Burke.

Pen and ink. 7¼×4¼ inches.

With Thackeray's instructions to the engraver. Bound in a copy of his *The Four Georges*, London 1861, facing the plate of Lord North and Mr Fox, p 147.

Lovel the Widower

68. Study for "I Am Referred to Cecelia."
Pencil. 6½×4½ inches.
Mounted and bound in a copy of his *Lovel the Widower*, London 1861, facing the corresponding plate, the frontispiece.

69. "I." Sketch for decorative initial.
Pencil. 2½×3 inches.
In autograph note to John Tenniel; [London, after 1861?]. With a proof of the engraving—reproduced lower right. Thackeray's instructions read: "Do do draw on a wood block an eagle for me with a broken wing covering over half a shield of stars and stripes—and oblige Your faithful WMT."

69

THE TRAVELER

THACKERAY, born in Calcutta, never lost his cosmopolitan character. Returning to England from India at the age of six he caught a glimpse of Napoleon at St Helena. Having lived in Paris, he knew the city intimately; he spoke French fluently and observed the French people closely. When circumstances forced him to earn a living it was the theatre-goer and ballet fan of Parisian days who supplied the material: stage sets and theatrical characters figure importantly in his early sketch books. At nineteen he traveled in Germany for nine months, reading German literature in Weimar, where he met Goethe.

Thackeray's early commercial assignments were travel articles, collected in *The Paris Sketch Book* (1840). In 1838 he had supplied illustrations for Charles Addison's *Damascus and Palmyra*, a travel book which was followed in 1846 by his own *Notes of a Journey from Cornhill to Grand Cairo*. An Irish visit in 1842 led to *The Irish Sketch-Book* (1843), and his German travels provided materials for *The Kickleburys on the Rhine* (1850). The writer who in *Vanity Fair* gave an unforgettable description of the Battle of Waterloo had obviously traveled in Belgium and Holland. Thackeray's Mediterranean tour of 1844 made him a popular tourist in Rome, where he spent the winter of 1854. The two lecture tours in the United States took him through the classic Grand American circuit; he developed a preference for the South which made him sympathetic to the Confederate cause at the beginning of the Civil War. By that time however Thackeray, whose life had been spent in the great world, had become preoccupied with London, his club, an opulent new home, and himself. The pen that had accompanied him on his travels was finally laid down on Christmas Eve 1863.

70. Thackeray the traveler.

Pen and ink. 2 × 2 ¾ inches.

Inscribed "Thackery [sic] delin." in an unidentified hand. On the half title of a copy of his *Notes of a Journey from Cornhill to Grand Cairo*, London 1846.

71. "I have been thinking of a walking trip for us two next year—about this time say."

Pen and ink; pen and ink with water color.

1 ½ × 1 ¾ inches; 2 ¼ × 7 ¼ inches.

In autograph letter to Edward Fitzgerald; [September 8–9 1831].

72. Jardin des Tuileries.

Pen and ink. 4×6 inches.

Signed with spectacles in the lower right corner. Mounted and bound in a copy of *The Students' Quarter or Paris Five-and-Thirty Years Since; By the Late William Makepeace Thackeray*, London [1874?], facing the corresponding plate, following p 56.

73. Study for "French Catholicism."

Pen and ink with water color. 6×4¼ inches.

Mounted and bound in a copy of his *The Paris Sketch Book*, v 2, London 1840, facing the corresponding plate, preceding p 105.

70

NOTES OF A JOURNEY

FROM

CORNHILL TO GRAND CAIRO.

74

74. Place de la Concorde.
Pencil. 8 × 5 inches.
Bound in Charles Dickens' copy of *Vanity Fair*,
London 1848, preceding the frontispiece.

75. French actors and character sketches.
Pen and ink with water color. 7 ¾ × 6 ¼ inches.
In an early sketchbook presented to Edward Fitzgerald, with captions in the hand of Mrs Carmichael-Smyth, Thackeray's mother.

76. "I have drawn you a view of a little street close
by, wʰ strikes me as very quiet & characteristic of
this dear old country of France. —What is more
there are actual nuns in this village, wʰ though
within the barrier is altogether countryfied . . . ."
Pen and ink with water color. 9 ¼ × 7 inches.
In autograph letter to Edward Fitzgerald; [May
1835].

77. "Here is a copy of a beautiful scene in a play
called Perrinet Le Clerc, wʰ they are now doing at
the Porte St. M: it is of course full of horrors &
adulteries; but the scenery & costumes are charm-
ing . . . ."
Pen and ink. 2 × 3 ¼ inches.
In autograph letter to Edward Fitzgerald; [Nov-
ember 22 1832].

78. "Mˡˡᵉ Atala Beauchêne."
Pen and ink with water color. 6 × 4 inches.

79. "T." Study for decorative initial.
Pencil. 5 ¼ × 4 inches.
With Thackeray's instructions to the engraver,
which read: "Please, Mr. Skill, make the letter
smaller if you can. Put the wheel right, plenty of
luggage on the roof, the gentleman a clergyman,
& the back of the one horse in the shafts."

A is a shining
metal box & cover

containing the compass

Note the boys very young & chubby

80. "On the Rhine Boat."

Pencil. 7½×4¾ inches.

Study for an illustration (unpublished) for *The Kickleburys on the Rhine*.

81. Study for "The Old Story."

Pencil with water color. 7½×4¾ inches.

Inscribed "From Lady Kicklebury on the Rhine" by Anne Thackeray, Lady Ritchie. Published in *The Kickleburys on the Rhine*, London 1850.

82. "You will remark my dear Lady Highdry, that the match was decidedly against *my* inclinations . . . ."

Pen and ink. 7¼×5¼ inches.

Study for an illustration (unpublished) for *The Kickleburys on the Rhine*, with a proof of the engraving.

83. Study for "Schlafen Sie wohl."

Pen and ink. 4¾× 7 inches.

Published in *The Kickleburys on the Rhine*.

84

84. Two studies for "Little Dutchmen."

Pencil. 3×2 inches (reproduced above); 7×4½ inches (reproduced on the preceding page).

Mounted and bound in a copy of his *Roundabout Papers; Reprinted from "The Cornhill Magazine,"* London 1863, facing the corresponding plate, preceding p 299. With Thackeray's instructions to the engraver, which read: "A is a shining metal box & cover containing the compass. Make the boys very young & chubby."

85. "Killarney Race Course. Playing a game at cards for 'half a sovereign.'" Study for the illustration accompanying the text ". . . here were a pair (indeed they are very good portraits) who came forward disinterestedly with a table and a pack of cards . . . ."

Pencil. 8¼×7 inches.

Published in *The Irish Sketch-Book*, London 1843.

86. Two drawings: a *contadina*; duelling figures.

Pencil. 7×3¾ inches; 7×3 inches.

In the margin and on the verso of the map of the Roman Forum in Thackeray's copy of *Information and Directions for Travellers on the Continent of Europe, More Particularly in Italy and in the Island of Sicily* by Mariana Starke, eighth edition, London 1832. This copy of Mariana Starke's standard guide bears the bookplate of Thackeray's stepfather, Henry Carmichael-Smyth; on the verso of the title page Thackeray has sketched himself as a tourist, perhaps while admiring the Forum.

87. Boys on a donkey.

Water color. 5×7 inches.

Sketch for an illustration (unpublished) for *Notes of a Journey from Cornhill to Grand Cairo*.

88. "Cairo."

Pencil with water color. 7×10 inches.

Sketch for an illustration (unpublished) for *Notes of a Journey from Cornhill to Grand Cairo*.

89. "Jerusalem"; "Jerusalem"; "Horseman at the Sepulcre[sic]"; "Beyrout."

Water color. 6¾×9¾ inches.

Signed at lower right. Sketches for illustrations (unpublished) for *Notes of a Journey from Cornhill to Grand Cairo*.

90

90. "At Constantinople." Study for "A Street View at Constantinople."

Water color. 4½×7¼ inches.

Published as the frontispiece of *Notes of a Journey from Cornhill to Grand Cairo*, London 1846.

91. Study for "A Street View at Constantinople."

Pencil. 3¾×5½ inches.

Mounted and bound in a copy of his *Notes of a Journey from Cornhill to Grand Cairo*, facing the corresponding plate, the frontispiece.

92. The Lord's Prayer in a circle the size of a threepenny piece. Dated 1861.

Pen and ink. ¾ inches in diameter.

In autograph note to Miss Gassiot.

PART II

William Blake to Denton Welch

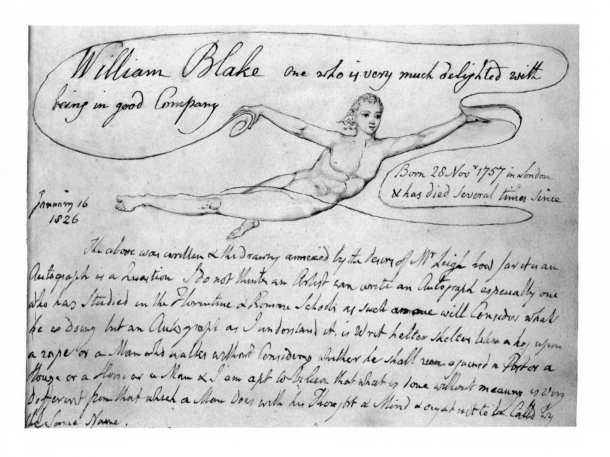

William Blake

(1757–1827)

93. "WILLIAM BLAKE one who is very much delighted with being in good company."

Pen and ink with wash. 3 × 8¼ inches.

Dated January 16 1826. On p 19 of v 2 of William Upcott's album, entitled by Upcott "Reliques of My Contemporaries . . . 1833."

No exhibition of artist-authors could be complete without an example from the hand of William Blake. This technical innovator and master of printmaking is perhaps the most influential figure in the development of the English print and is of major importance in the English literary tradition. Disclaiming the simple signature as impossible for an artist "who has Studied in the Florentine & Roman Schools," Blake wrote in the album of the librarian-antiquary William Upcott that his autograph should be classed with "Works of Art & not of Nature or Chance."

Elizabeth Barrett Browning
(1806–1861)

94. Flush, the poet's spaniel.

Pen and ink. 2 × 2 ½ inches.

On inside front cover of her manuscript poetry notebook signed and dated 1843.

Some dogs have greatness thrust upon them. One such was Flush, whose portrait was sketched by his mistress and whose biography, written by Virginia Woolf, appeared in 1933.

94

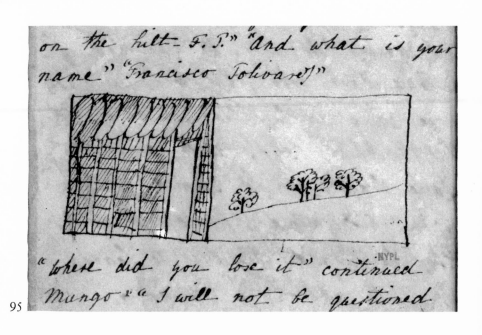

95

There was an old man whose Giardino
Produced only one little bean o'.
When he said — "That' enough!" — They answered "What stuff!
You never can live on one bean o'!

96

Alfred, Lord Tennyson
(1809–1892)

95. Mungo's hut.

Pen and ink. 1 ½ × 3 ¾ inches.

On p [6] of the manuscript of his "Mungo the American; A Tale" dated 1823.

Lord Tennyson's earliest prose work, written when he was fourteen and presented by him to his governess, contains this sketch by the future poet who was to prove himself an accomplished draughtsman.

Edward Lear
(1812–1888)

96. "There was an old man whose Giardino . . . ."

Pen and ink. 5 × 7 ¾ inches.

One of six illustrated limericks inserted in a copy of his *A Book of Nonsense*, eighth edition, London [1864?].

This unpublished sketch reflects the total Lear: artist and traveler as well as rhymer and tutor for Lord Derby's grandchildren.

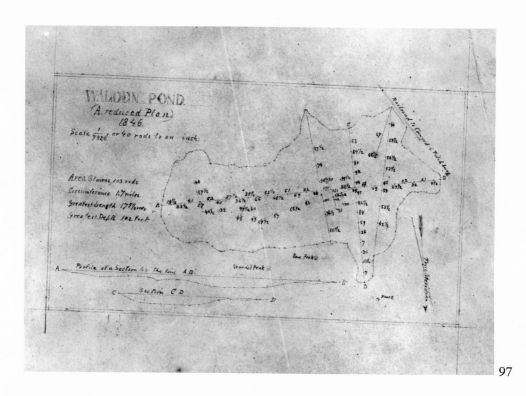

97

Henry David Thoreau
(1817–1862)

97. "Walden Pond. (A reduced Plan.) 1846."
Pencil. 7×9¾ inches.

"As I was desirous to recover the long lost bottom of Walden Pond, I surveyed it carefully, before the ice broke up, early in '46 . . . ." This is Thoreau's original drawing of that survey, an engraving from which was published in his *Walden* (Boston 1854). He supported himself by surveying land and by making pencils in his father's shop. One such pencil is on exhibit.

98

34

Charlotte and Emily Brontë
(1816–1855)   (1818–1848)

98. Charlotte Brontë. Classical ruins.
Pencil. 2×3½ inches.
Signed with initials in the lower left corner and dated May 20 1829. On p [3] of the manuscript of her "The Keep of the Bridge."

99. Charlotte Brontë. Classical figure.
Water color. 7½×4¾ inches.
Dated November 26 1830.

100. Emily Brontë. "Forget Me Not."
Water color. 9¾×7½ inches.

The Brontë children wrote stories in an infinitesimal script for each other's delight, and from one of these comes Charlotte's drawing of classical ruins. Charlotte and Emily also copied biblical scenes, Byronic characters, and landscapes from Annuals, those enormously popular compilations of belles lettres and the visual arts that so delighted the nineteenth century.

John Ruskin
(1819–1900)

101. "We have been since 5th July living in this kind of house . . . ."
Pen and ink. 3×5 inches.
In autograph letter to Frederick James Furnivall; Glenfinlus, [Scotland], October 16 [1853].
John Ruskin describes his role as taskmaster to Sir John Everett Millais, who in a location marked "A" in this sketch had been painting a torrent among rocks "which will make a revolution in landscape painting . . . ." Ruskin's correspondent was one of the founders of the London Workingmen's College and an early editor of what later was to become the Oxford English Dictionary.

102. "Abingdon."
Pencil. 5½×8¾ inches.
Signed and dated 1872.
During his tenure as the first Slade Professor of fine art at Oxford, Ruskin took his students out to show them how to sketch from nature. This drawing was made during one of the excursions to Abingdon.

101

Charles Godfrey Leland
(1824–1903)

103. "The History of Peter Curious Who Worried People to Death with Questions."
Pen and ink with water color. Thirteen leaves, each 8 ½ × 5 inches.

This sad tale is preserved on the versos of printed subscription notices issued at the New York office of the *Knickerbocker Magazine*. It is a prime example of the burlesque penmanship of the editor of *Vanity Fair* and creator of the character Hans Breitmann.

Lewis Carroll
(1832–1898)

104. Untitled series of cartoon drawings.
Pen and ink. One leaf (recto and verso), 11 ¼ × 13 inches.

Probably drawn for the amusement of children, this story in cartoon recalls the fact that the original manuscript of *Alice's Adventures Under Ground* was embellished by the storyteller himself.

103

105. Edith Caroline Morley.
Pencil. 7 × 5 ¾ inches.

Professor Henry Morley's daughter was digging on the sands at Sandown, Isle of Wight, when the mathematician of Christ Church, Oxford, drew her portrait. Morley received the sketch, a reminder of Carroll's abiding affection for little girls, with an accompanying note.

Mark Twain
(1835–1910)

106. Illustrated lecture notes.
Pen and ink. 7 × 4 ½ inches.
Inscribed "We're done with *this*, Charles, forever! Yrs MARK TWAIN." Dated "Liverpool, Jan. 9, 1874. 10^{30} P M."

Mark Twain was in the habit of using rough notes and sketches during his extensive lecture tours. Those on exhibit were sent to Charles Warren Stoddard at the end of an English tour. Isabel Lyon,

Mark Twain's secretary, annotated a photostat (also on view) interpreting the cryptic Western symbols as deciphered by W. L. Broun.

John Burroughs
(1837–1921)

107. Marginal sketches, including "Ye Pedagogue."
Pencil. 6 × 3 ¾ inches.
On inside back cover of "*A Note Book* Containing a few smooth pebbles, which the waves of Thought leave, from time to time upon my Shores. April 1859."

One would expect a naturalist, and furthermore one who inscribes his notebook in the fashion of a naturalist, to draw flowers, shells, or "smooth pebbles." It is all the more interesting to find that Burroughs decorated his notebook with faces and "Ye Pedagogue."

Thomas Hardy
(1840–1928)

108. "S. Juliot [before restoration]."
Pencil with water color. 10 × 12 inches.
Dated 1870.

108

109. "S. Juliot" [churchyard].
Pencil with water color. 10 × 12 inches.

110. " 'St. Neightan's Kieve' nr. Tintagel, Cornwall. Sketched on the spot by T. H."
Pencil. 5 ½ × 2 ½ inches.
Dated October 1871.

111. "Sketches made in the Vallency Valley. Boscastle, Cornwall."

Pencil. 4 × 3 ¾ inches.

Signed on the mat and dated 1870–1872.

Thomas Hardy, the son of a builder, was trained as an architect. The last major assignment he undertook before turning novelist was the restoration of the church of St Juliot in Cornwall. The view of the church before restoration has the quality of a professional elevation; the sketches of the Cornish countryside are of a more occasional nature.

111

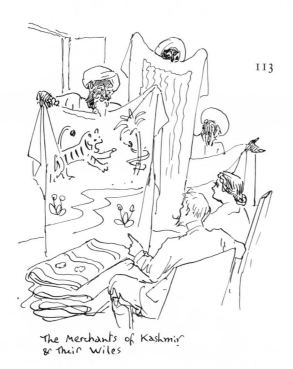

113

*The Merchants of Kashmir
& their Wiles*

Walter Crane
(1845–1915)

112. "Lahore—Waza Khan Mosque—Jan. 16, 1907."

Water color. 14 ½ × 10 inches.

Signed with initials in the lower left corner. Reproduced in black and white opposite p 182 of his *India Impressions*, London 1907.

113. "The Merchants of Kashmir & their Wiles."
Pen and ink. 8 × 4 ¾ inches.

On p [34] of the notebook "Our little Tour in India . . . A series of pen & ink sketches . . . ." Reproduced on p. 182 of *India Impressions*.

114. Corresponding page [155] of the manuscript of *India Impressions*, to which is attached a proof of the pen and ink sketch (item 113).

When artist-illustrator Walter Crane traveled in India, it was natural enough that he should record his impressions in ink and in water color. The trip turned him into an author as well for he later published his travel diary under the title *India Impressions*.

Kate Greenaway
(1846–1901)

115. Figure of a girl.
Pencil with water color. 2 × 2 ¼ inches.

Signed at the upper right and dated 1890. On the half title of John F. Dexter's copy of her *Under the Window*, London [1880?].

116. Girl on a donkey. Study for the illustration appearing on p 119 of *Topo* by G. E. Brunefille [Gertrude Blood, later Lady Colin Campbell], London 1878.

Pen and ink with water color. 4 ¼ × 5 ¼ inches.
Signed with initials in the lower right corner.

117. Preliminary sketch for the illustration appearing on p 119 of *Topo*.
Pencil. 6 ½ × 5 inches.

One of fifty-four drawings interleaved in Frederick Locker-Lampson's copy of *Topo*, London 1880.

For Kate Greenaway 1878 was a triumphant year. *Under the Window*, her first collection of verses and drawings, appeared under the aegis of Edmund Evans, one of the great wood-engravers and printers of his time and the principal supporter of Wal-

122 (detail)

ter Crane and Randolph Caldecott. It was an immediate best seller; and before the year was out further success came with Miss Greenaway's illustrations for *Topo*, which was written by a fifteen-year-old who was to become a peeress.

Julian Hawthorne
(1846–1934)

118. Portrait of Nathaniel Hawthorne.

Pencil. 7 × 5 inches.

Julian Hawthorne, who gained popular success with his melodramatic novels, is best remembered as the family chronicler. This sensitive pencil sketch of his father has the immediacy of a portrait from life.

Eugene Field
(1850–1895)

119. "Fred and His Firecracker."

Pen and ink with water color. 1 × 3 ¾ inches.

At head of autograph letter to Hildegarde Hawthorne; Kansas City, July 1 1889.

The interest in calligraphy which influenced the form of his printed work, and the charm of his talents as an occasional artist, are clearly evident in this decorated initial and whimsical headpiece by Eugene Field.

Lafcadio Hearn
(1850–1904)

120. Decorated title page of the manuscript of Lafcadio Hearn's English translation of *Avatar* by Théophile Gautier, dated 1878.

Pen and India ink. 8 ½ × 6 ¼ inches.

It is clear from marginalia in letters and decorated title pages that Hearn had a way with the brush; whether the brush work of Japanese artists may have influenced this emigrant from America who lived in the Orient for fourteen years is more difficult to determine.

A ROAD IN
KERRY.

AUGUST
1923 ═

123

Bernard Shaw

(1856–1950)

121. Self-portrait.

Pen and ink. 4 ½ × 3 ¼ inches.

122. Sheet of sketches including two self-caricatures.

Pen and ink. 8 × 5 inches.

On verso of shorthand holograph poem to Pakenham Beatty dated January 1 1882.

123. "A Road in Kerry. August 1923."

Pen and ink. 5 × 8 inches.

124. Self-portrait.

Water color. 8 ½ × 5 ½ inches.

125. Sketches for the statue of Saint Joan at Ayot St Lawrence.

Water color. 8 ½ × 11 inches.

With p 22 of *Bernard Shaw's Rhyming Picture Guide to Ayot Saint Lawrence*, Luton 1950.

As a matter of fact I am an artist to my finger tips, and always contend that I am a highly educated person because I had continual contacts with literature and art, including music, in my childhood, and found school and its Latin and Greek grind nothing but a brutalizing imprisonment which interfered disastrously with my real education.

BERNARD SHAW TO VIRGINIA WOOLF
May 10 1940

It is a little-known fact that Bernard Shaw had for three years (1886–1889) been art critic on the London *World* before his two years as music critic on the *Star* (1888–1890). In addition to critical acumen he had considerable facility with the draughtsman's pen, and a pronounced obsession: Bernard Shaw. His occupations and avocations were exceptionally diverse, and Bernard Shaw, the actor, had a demonstrably intimate knowledge of his own face—self-caricatures appear in multiple media and many contexts. Bernard Shaw, the stage and costume designer, is represented in the exhibition by his studies for a statue of Saint Joan. A page from the *Rhyming Picture Guide to Ayot Saint Lawrence* shows the work, as executed by sculptor Clare Winsten, in the garden of Shaw's home.

This little sketch was done by
Joseph Conrad in his rooms
in Wilton Road Victoria in
1896. To show me how the girls
for the ballet were engaged.

126

Joseph Conrad
(1857–1924)

126. Six drawings of women.

Pen and colored inks. Each 7×4½ inches.
Dated 1892–1896 by Jessie Conrad.

The seaman is observant by nature, the novelist by profession. Pictures so vivid may well be worth a thousand words, even those of such a consummate verbal artist as Joseph Conrad. Conrad recorded persons he observed engaged in their daily activities, as those on exhibit, and also had the habit of setting down his visual image of characters from his novels.

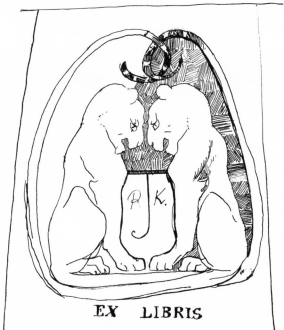

127

EX LIBRIS

129

Rudyard Kipling
(1865–1936)

127. "Tied up in tails! (or tales) or is it tales of tails?" Two studies for his bookplate with initials J R K.

Pen and India ink. 17¼×6½ inches.

128. "Inspiration." Sheet of self-caricatures; and another version.

Pen and India ink. 8½×13½ inches;
3¾×3¼ inches.

129. "The Birthday of Madame Cigale." Sketch for title page; with separate sketch of standing figure.

Pen and India ink. 7½×6 inches (reproduced at left); 6½×3¼ inches.

130. "The Bull that Meant no Harm. Or How the Best Handmade Split Bamboo Rod Was Lost." Series of cartoon drawings.

Pen and ink. 3 p, each 9¼×5¾ inches.
In Florence Garrard's sketchbook.

131. "The City of Dreadfull [sic] Night. By Rudyard Kipling." Decorated title page of the manuscript.
Pen and ink. 8½×6¾ inches.
Manuscript dated January–February 1888.

132. "Ho-Twang—The Musician" and "Howlee the Singer."
Pen and ink. One leaf (recto and verso), 5×3¾ inches.

133. "Arrangement in Impossibilities."
Pen and ink. 3¼×6½ inches.
Signed "K. del." at lower center.

134. Grotesque figure.
Pen and ink. 3¾×3¾ inches, with description on verso.
Signed "K. del." at lower center.

135. Three drawings of Eastern figures.
Pen and ink. 8½×6½ inches; 7×5 inches; 8×4 inches.

136. "Herba panisclavus fata. Suprema cinis. W. Raleigh."

Pen and ink. 6½×6¼ inches.
Signed "Jaye. Arre. Kaye." in the lower right corner.

137. "Writings and Songs by J. R. K." Decorated verso of the free end paper and the title page for the manuscript notebook.
Pen and ink. 6¼×7½ inches.
Dated 1882.

138. A departing carriage.
Pen and ink. 4¼×4 inches.
On p 73 of the manuscript notebook "Departmental Ditties. And Other Verses. Written in '81.'"

Those who have read Rudyard Kipling's *Just So Stories* in an edition illustrated with the author's drawings are unlikely to forget either the stories or the pictures. His clever pen wrought verbal and visual magic not only for publication, but also on the pages of his working manuscripts, in sketchbooks, and on random slips of paper carefully preserved by admirers. The clarity of his flowing line and his subtle use of stark blacks balanced against white space create effects similar to those of Aubrey Beardsley, whose work matured in a later decade.

133

131

Château de Psaux
9 Sept 1905
u b ...

139

141

Arnold Bennett
(1867–1931)

139. "Chateau de Penne."
Charcoal. 7¾×6¼ inches.
Dated September 9 1908. In his "Journal Volume Nine . . . Midi," dated 1908.

140. Garden landscape.
Charcoal. 7¾×5¾ inches.
Dated August 1 1908. In his "Journal Vol. Ten. Switzerland & England," dated 1908–1909.

141. View of the Promenade at Brighton.
Pencil with crayon. 6¼×7¾ inches.
In his "Journal Volume 12a," dated "about 1909."

142. "La Badia."
Pencil with crayon. 7×4¼ inches.
Dated April 12 1910. In his "Journal Vol. 13 . . . Florence," dated 1910.

143. Sailing.
Pencil. 7×4¼ inches.
In his "Journal Volume XIV . . . France," dated 1910.

The traveler's journal is an ideal medium for a natural diarist with strong inclinations toward landscape painting. In the volumes of his journal, thirty-five of which are in the Berg Collection, Arnold Bennett recorded with pen, pencil, and crayon, and often in the manner of the Impressionist painters, his travels in Italy, Switzerland, and the South of France.

144

George Russell (Æ)
(1867–1935)

144. Self-portrait, with marginal sketches of W. B. Yeats, John O'Leary, Edward Martyn, and G. K. Chesterton.

Pencil with pen and ink. 7¾×5¼ inches.

Signed with initials "Æ" at lower right of self-portrait.

145. View in Ballymore, Co Donegal.

Pen and ink with crayon. 4×6½ inches.

In autograph letter to W. T. H. Howe; Ballymore, [Ireland], June 20 1934.

146. Portrait of James Stephens.

Charcoal. 14×10 inches.

Inscribed "A E to W H T [sic] Howe" in the lower right corner and dated September 13 1920.

147. Portrait of John Butler Yeats.

Pencil. 10×7 inches.

Inscribed "J B Yeats by his victim A.E" in the lower right corner.

148. View of mountains.

Pen and ink with crayon. 2½×4¼ inches.

Signed with initials "A E" in the lower left corner. On title page of Diarmuid Russell's copy of *Collected Poems by A.E.*, London 1926, with ninety-one drawings by George Russell added by him for presentation to his son.

Æ was a natural painter whose achievements in the world of letters bear evidence of the colorist-draughtsman's perception. Editor of the *Irish Homestead* (1906–1923), leading figure in the social and political ferment of his time, and one of the half-dozen major personalities of the Irish Literary Revival, Russell found time in his full life to produce a continuing flow of realistic portraits and lyrical landscapes in the Romantic manner.

Max Beerbohm
(1872–1956)

149. "Thia and Thol—B.C. 39,000." Study for the frontispiece of his *The Dreadful Dragon of Hay Hill*, London 1928.

Pen and ink with water color. 11¾×7½ inches.

Signed "Max 1928" in the lower right corner.

150. "[Bernard Shaw] The Socialist."

Oil and water color with pencil. 8¾×6 inches.

Doctored photographic plate facing p 116 in his copy of *George Bernard Shaw* by Archibald Henderson, London 1911.

151. Self-portrait with other sketches.

Pencil. 15×11 inches.

The *enfant terrible* of Edwardian England was undoubtedly "Max" the artist. His sketches and captions lampooned English history and literature from the images of 39,000 B.C. to the productions of "Max" himself. Books from Sir Max Beerbohm's library carry the marks of the poison pen he deftly wielded to deflate the pomposity of contemporaries enshrined in authorized biographies.

152

G. K. Chesterton
(1874–1936)

152. Enraged gentleman and his victim.
Pencil. 2 p, each 9×7 inches.
On p [58] and [59] of an early sketchbook.

The creator of Father Brown was a student at the Slade School of Art, and sufficiently talented to have made a reputation for himself as an artist. The sketchbook exhibited dates from Chesterton's early twenties. In addition to quick pencil portrait sketches it contains drawings intended as illustrations for a story, as can be seen by notes for chapter headings and a list of "Dramatis Personae."

Maurice Baring
(1874–1945)

153. Wedding of Princess Forget-Me-Not and Prince Lily-of-the-Valley.
Pencil with water color. 10¼×8 inches.

On p [2] of a copy of his *La Princesse Myosotis et le Prince Muguet* [n p, n d].

When privileged children illustrate a story, they do so in an edition their mothers have had privately printed. Maurice Baring's governess, Chérie, described on the title page as The Queen of Beauty, told her charge this tale. Baring, described on the title page as Her Husband, added illustrations.

John Masefield
(1878–1967)

154. Sailing vessel.
Pen and ink. 3×3 inches.

155. Sailing vessel.
Pen and colored inks. 1½×2½ inches.

In his "Book of the Model Mast," manuscript notebook written for David Scott, and dated November 22 1909.

156. "Rupert's grave Sept. 11th. 5:30 pm. 1915."

Pencil with water color. 3 1/4 × 4 1/2 inches.
Enclosed in a letter to Sir Edward Marsh; Lemnos, [Greece], September 11 and 12 1915.

The poet of *Salt Water Ballads* never lost his love of the sea, nor the sailor his knowledge of ships; and Masefield the draughtsman constantly drew ships. While serving in the Red Cross during the First World War, Masefield made for Sir Edward Marsh a quick sketch of the Isle of Skyros, drawn in "a freak . . . light." Here Rupert Brooke, whose friendship Masefield and Sir Edward shared, had come to his grave less than six months before.

157

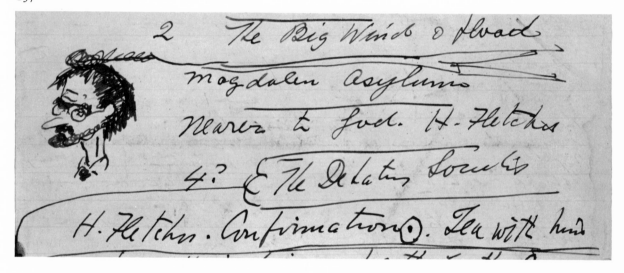

Sean O'Casey
(1884–1964)

157. Self-portrait.
Pen and ink. 1 1/2 × 1 1/4 inches.
On p [42] of a manuscript draft of his *Pictures in the Hallway.*

158. Stage setting.
Pencil. 2 1/2 × 5 1/4 inches.
In manuscript notes and dialogue for his *The Silver Tassie.*

159. "St. Donat's Castle, Glamorgan. Great Hall."
Pencil. 8 1/2 × 5 1/2 inches.
On p [80] of the manuscript notebook containing a draft of his *The Star Turns Red* and "R.I.P." from *I Knock at the Door.*

Sean O'Casey the man was usually seen "under a colored cap." On rare instances, Sean O'Casey the author drew his own capless portrait. More frequently, Sean O'Casey the dramatist sketched stage sets and interiors in working notebooks.

160 (detail)

Ronald Firbank
(1886–1926)

160. Characters from *Valmouth*.

Pencil. 2 p, each 6¼×4 inches.

In the manuscript notebook containing notes for his *The Princess Zoubaroff* and *Valmouth*.

The notebook is opened to fantastical sketches of characters from *Valmouth*. The haloed figure at her devotions may well be Sister Ecclesia, whom "strangers sometimes took . . . to be a saint, in touch with heaven." *Vis à vis*, demurely *recherché*, is Mrs Hurstpierpont, who in the novel sighs "Ah Ingres . . . your portrait of me is still indeed most like . . . ." Firbank has annotated the sketch: "How Ingres admired my hands —He quite worshiped [sic] my little fingers—"

Siegfried Sassoon
(1886–1967)

161. "Via Crucis." Illustrated poem.
Pencil with colored inks. 7 ×9 inches.

162. "Portrait of the Author as a child."
Ink block-prints on rice paper.
On verso of the half title of his own copy of his *Counter-Attack*, London 1918.

No poet has voiced the objections against war as seen from the trenches with more painful beauty than Siegfried Sassoon.

> Night & rain, and misery and blood . . .
> Mangling crumps, and bullets thro' the brain . . .
> Night conceals us with a soaking scud—

are lines from the poem "Via Crucis" sent to Sir Edward Marsh effectively illustrated to catch the mood of night and rain and misery and despair. The poet's corrected copy of his volume of war poems is opened to a curiously oblique self-portrait.

Isaac Rosenberg
(1890–1918)

163. View of trees and houses.
Pencil with water color. 5 ×7 inches.
The artistic genius of the young poet Isaac Rosenberg is indicated in this quick sketch sent to his patron, Sir Edward Marsh. Rosenberg had formal training in art at the Slade School, and had developed an individual poetic voice before his death at twenty-eight in the First World War.

Henry Miller
(1891–   )

164. Self-portrait.
Pencil with pen and India ink. 11 ¾×9 ¼ inches.
Signed at lower center and dated August 1946. Decorated wrapper for the corrected typescript of his *Remember to Remember*.

Henry Miller characteristically portrays himself in narrative and pictorial fashion. In a note accompanying this typescript he remarks, "If I had a 'sav-

ing and keeping' nature, this is one document I should like to have 'preserved for the archives'. . . ."

Enid Bagnold
(1889–   )

165. Portrait of Claud Lovat Fraser.
Crayon. 4 ×3 ½ inches.
Inscribed "July, 1912. Me by Enid.   L.F." in the lower right corner. Mounted under a drawing by Fraser on the free end paper of a copy of *The Beggar's Opera; Written by Mr. Gay* [Scenes and Costumes by C. Lovat Fraser], London 1921.

166. "London [to] Vienna."
Pen and ink with water color. 6 ½×4 inches.
Inscribed "To Mr. Clement Shorter—1920" and signed at the center right. On the verso of the series notice in a copy of her *A Diary Without Dates*, London 1918.

Enid Bagnold, Lady Jones, studied drawing and painting with Walter Sickert when she was a young woman. Her friendship with the artist Lovat Fraser dates from this period. In the pictorial itinerary sketched on a blank introductory page of her first book, Miss Bagnold condensed into pen strokes the journey described in thousands of words on the pages that follow.

Stephen Spender
(1909–   )

167. Occasional sketches.
Pencil with pen and ink. 2 p, each 11 ¾×8 inches.
On the end papers of his manuscript poetry notebook dated 1961–1963.

These obscure drawings mirror that "excess of ideas and . . . weak sense of form" in his writing upon which Stephen Spender has self-critically commented.

164

169

George Barker
(1913–   )

169. Landscape.

Pencil with ball-point pens. 8 ½ × 5 inches.
On p [12] of his manuscript notebook for *Dreams of a Summer Night*.

Contrary to popular opinion, great writers do not necessarily have illegible hands. Some of the most beautiful scripts belong to eminent authors, and in the case of George Barker penmanship in the best calligraphic tradition is coupled with a flowing line often seen in the embellishment of his notebooks.

Dylan Thomas
(1914–1953)

170. Self-caricature.

Pencil. 8 ¼ × 5 inches.
One of four sketches in Pamela Phillips' copy of his *The Map of Love*, London 1939.

In pubs and in company, in Wales and in London, the poet turned cartoonist. This drawing and its companion pieces, which include a sketch of Caitlin Thomas, were executed in November 1943, in the Wheatsheaf Tavern, London.

Denton Welch
(1915–1948)

171. Pedestal table.

Pen and ink. 2 ¾ × 1 ½ inches.
In autograph letter to Peggy Kirkaldy; Tonbridge, [England], January 31 1946.

172. Ornamental sketches.

Pen and ink. 5 ½ × 3 inches.
Inscribed "It was in the April of 1943." On verso of unmailed envelope.

Denton Welch was an invalid for years before his death, the result of a bicycle accident he had suffered at the age of twenty. It had been his ambition to become a painter; and these sketches give some idea of the draughtsmanship of the young man best remembered for his novelistic portrayal of childhood and crippled adolescence.

William Sansom
(1912–   )

168. "It's not my fault."

Felt-tip pen. 4 × 10 inches.
Signed with initials in the lower right corner.

William Sansom's ability to give sensual reality to narrative event took a whimsical turn in his illustrations for *The Get-well-quick Colouring Book* and *Who's Zoo*. This line drawing from a sketchbook given by the author to his wife, Ruth, has a characteristic immediacy.

170

ACKNOWLEDGMENTS

THE COMPILERS of this catalogue express their thanks to Miss Marion Kahn who in her capacity as assistant in the Berg Collection has been unfailingly helpful in major and minor emergencies.

We wish to thank Mrs Edward Norman Butler for her kind permission to reproduce the illustrations by William Makepeace Thackeray which are published for the first time in this catalogue. Thackeray's self-caricature from Lady Rachel Russell's copy of *The Kickleburys on the Rhine*, his portrait of Isabella Shawe Thackeray, and the sketch of Thackeray the traveler, which were published in Gordon Ray's *Thackeray:* I *The Uses of Adversity*, II *The Age of Wisdom* (New York 1955–1958), are reproduced with the permission of the McGraw-Hill Book Company. The sketches "My foot was actually uplifted to quit the shore of Albion . . ." and the drawings of the Messenger delivering a letter to Dr Primrose and of the Lord's Prayer in a circle the size of a threepenny piece have previously been reproduced in Professor Ray's *The Letters and Private Papers of William Makepeace Thackeray* (4 vols Cambridge 1945–1946), published by Harvard University Press.

For permission to reproduce the illustrations in this catalogue, we are grateful to the following: to Mr John Murray, for the drawing by Elizabeth Barrett Browning; to Charles, Lord Tennyson, for the sketch by Alfred, Lord Tennyson; to George Allen & Unwin Ltd, for the drawing by John Ruskin; to Mrs Grace Collingwood, for the sketch by Lewis Carroll; to the Trustees of the Estate of Thomas Hardy, for the drawings by Thomas Hardy; to the Society of Authors as Agent for the Estate of Bernard Shaw, for the sketches by Bernard Shaw; to the Trustees of the Joseph Conrad Estate and to J. M. Dent & Sons Ltd, for the drawing by Joseph Conrad; to Mrs George Bambridge, for the drawings by Rudyard Kipling; to Mrs Dorothy Cheston-Bennett, for the drawings by Arnold Bennett; to Mr Diarmuid Russell, for the self-portrait by George Russell; to Dorothy E. Collins, Literary Executor of the G. K. Chesterton Estate, for the sketch by G. K. Chesterton; to Mrs Sean O'Casey, for the sketches by Sean O'Casey; to Colonel Thomas Firbank, for the sketch by Ronald Firbank; to Mr Henry Miller, for his self-portrait; to Mr George Barker, for his landscape drawing; to the Trustees for the Copyright of Dylan Thomas, for the sketch by Dylan Thomas.

INDEX TO AUTHORS AND ILLUSTRATIONS

Numbers refer to pages; italic numbers refer to page numbers of illustrations.

This book was designed by Roderick Stinehour
and set in Bembo type at The Stinehour Press, Lunenburg, Vermont.
Two thousand copies were printed by offset lithography
on Mohawk Superfine paper at
The Meriden Gravure Company,
Meriden, Connecticut.

92